STOCK MARKET INVESTING

For Beginners

Discover How to Have Success in the Stock Market, Improve Your Health and Become Free With the Moore Trading Method

Robert Winston Moore Jr.

Robert W. Moore Jr.
Trading Method

©Copyright 2020

TABLE OF CONTENTS

INTRODUCTION..1
CHAPTER 1: WHY SHOULD YOU START INVESTING IN THE STOCK MARKET? 3

    Beats Inflation 4
    Has the Power of Compounding 6
    Easy to Invest 6
    Diversification 7

CHAPTER 2: FUNDAMENTALS OF THE STOCK MARKET 9

    What Is the Stock Market?...9
    Investing vs. Trading 11
    Understand the Risk Involved 12
    Participants of the Stock Market..................................13
    Primary and Secondary Markets...................................18
    Important Terms Related to the Stock Market...............19

CHAPTER 3: A STEP-BY-STEP GUIDE TO START INVESTING IN STOCKS 25

    Step 1 – Determine What Your Goals Are 26
    Step 2 – Educate Yourself About the Stock Market........ 28
    Step 3 – Always Have a Cash Reserve...........................29
    Step 4 – Start By Opening a Retirement Account 30
    Step 5 – Choose a Low-Cost Online Service 31
    Step 6 – Start By Investing in ETFs or Mutual Funds.....32
    Step 7 – Stick With Index Funds..................................33
    Step 8 – Use Dollar-Cost Averaging..............................34
    Step 9 – Slowly Start Investing in Individual Stocks.......36
    Step 10 – Always Diversify..37

CHAPTER 4: CAN YOU INVEST IN STOCKS WITH A LOW INVESTMENT? 38

    Invest Your Spare Change...39
    Use an Online Broker... 41
    Invest in a Retirement Plan Sponsored By Your Employer44

CHAPTER 5: TIPS TO CHOOSE THE RIGHT BROKER 47

    Understand Your Needs.. 48
    Narrow Down the Options 49
    Enquire About the Fees 52
    Test the Platform 53

Check the Reliability of the Customer Service 54
The Online Broker Platform Should Be User-Friendly.... 56

CHAPTER 6: HOW TO EARN REGULAR INCOME THROUGH STOCK MARKET INVESTING? 58

Research Quality Stocks 59
Look At the Stock's Quote 62
Purchase the Stock 63
Keep Track of Your Dividends 64
Manage Your Investment Funds 65

CHAPTER 7: AN INTRODUCTION TO DAY TRADING AND SWING TRADING 69

Who Is a Day Trader? 70
What Is Swing Trading? 70
Day Trading vs. Swing Trading 71
Day Trading Restrictions That You Should Know About 80
All That You Need to Know About Paper Trading 83

CHAPTER 8: HOW TO MAKE A TRADE? 85

Steps To Follow for Your First Trade 87
Create a Trading Routine 91

CHAPTER 9: RISK MANAGEMENT AND TRADING PSYCHOLOGY 96

Types of Risk 97
Risk Management Strategies That You Should Know ... 102
Steps to Master Trading Psychology 107

CHAPTER 10: MISTAKES THAT YOU SHOULD AVOID 113

No Basic Knowledge 114
Investing In An Industry You Don't Know About 115
Having Too High Expectations 116
Investing With the Mindset of a Trader 118
Becoming Emotionally Associated With a Company 120
Investing Money That Is Too Important to Lose 121
Not Diversifying Enough 122
Buying Shares On Credit 123

CONCLUSION 125

INTRODUCTION

Congratulations on purchasing *Stock Market Investing for Beginners,* and thank you for doing so.

The stock market is a place where everyone wants to invest their money in the hope of some handsome returns. But there are a lot of things that you need to learn before you embark on this journey, and in this book, you are going to learn all of those fundamentals that are going to prepare you for what lies ahead. People who invest in the market randomly thinking that it depends on luck are the ones that lose a lot of money.

The stock market is definitely a good option if you want to beat inflation, and when properly understood, the market can really be on your side. But if you are going to invest in the market simply after hearing from your friends and colleagues that a certain stock is performing well, then you are in for some setbacks because the first rule of making a profit in stocks is that you should never jump into it blindly. In this book, I have outlined the chapters in a lucid language so that even a beginner without any prior knowledge can understand it in one go. Once you have completed this book, you will be able to treat the stock market as a money-making machine, but first, you need patience and the ability to make smart choices.

There are plenty of books on this subject on the market, thanks again for choosing this one! Every effort was made to ensure it is full of as much useful information as possible, please enjoy! Leave me a quick review if you like it, it's important for me to know what you think.

Chapter 1:
WHY SHOULD YOU START INVESTING IN THE STOCK MARKET?

If you want to increase your wealth, then the stock market is definitely what you should choose for. If you are nervous about it, it's quite normal, and you don't have to worry so much because, in this chapter, I am going to show you the reasons why you should invest in the market. It's true that the stock market is unpredictable, but there are several strategies that you can use to make a probable prediction and people are earning huge amounts of money through the same strategies. How you perceive the stock market to be is one of the greatest reasons behind you feeling reluctant to invest in it, but I am sure that once you go through this chapter, your perception is going to change.

Whether you are saving for your retirement or you are saving for your dream house, whatever your ultimate goal is, the stock market can be a good place to save that amount of money.

Here are some of the reasons why I consider stocks as a relatively more viable investment for wealth generation.

Beats Inflation

If you are trying to save your money in the hope that after about ten years, you are going to have a huge chunk in your hand, then your worst enemy in this journey is going to be inflation. The United States has had an inflation rate of 3%, so where does it leave you? If your money is sitting idle in a savings account or a CD (certificate of deposit), inflation can reduce its value by great numbers. In order to keep up with the rate of inflation, that money would have to increase by at least 3%. Now, you must be thinking, what about the interest? Well, you are not going to get more than 2% even if you have opened a high-yield savings account.

In the case of CDs, the interest rate is slightly more than that of savings accounts, and that is why you might be able to keep up with the rate of inflation slightly more than that of savings accounts, but there are other disadvantages in the case of CD. For example, let us say your CD is for a period of 10 years and you decide to withdraw your money before that, then a huge amount is deducted as a penalty for early withdrawal.

But in the case of the stock market, if you learn all the tactics and strategies and do it right, you will stand a chance to grow your wealth by as much as 7-10% every year when considered over the long-term. So, suppose you have invested an amount of $10,000, and considering the fact that the rate of interest is somewhere around 7% every year, you will soon have $20,000 in your hands by the end of a span of 10 years. Imagine your money growing from $10,000 to $20,000 just because you invested it in stocks a decade earlier. And if you are good with savings, then you can invest $10,000 every year and earn huge profits. In the same way, you will have somewhere around $300,000 of money invested over a period of 30 years, that is, $10,000 every year. Do you know how much profit you will have at the end of 30 years if the interest rate is roughly around 7%? It will become $1,010,730! So, you will now be a millionaire. If we break it up, then the net profit that you gained over a period of 30 years is $710,730, and your investment was only $300,000.

Has the Power of Compounding

There is a reason why financial advisors will tell you to start saving from as early on in life as possible. For example, if your savings are steady, then you can invest in stocks and take advantage of its power of compounding. In the previous section, I showed you how your money would grow in 30 years, but do you know how much potential of growth it has when you think about the next 60 years? Considering that the interest would still remain to be roughly 7%, at the end of 60 years, your money will become $8,104,668. Yes, that is how money compounds when you invest it in stocks! When you have saved your money, you definitely wouldn't want it to lose its money over time just because it was sitting idle in your savings account, right? So, you need to start learning about the fundamentals and invest in the stock market right away!

Easy to Invest

Whoever told you that the stock market is hard to understand, did not really understand it themselves or they were on the wrong side of it because investing in stocks is pretty easy. All you have to do is research the online brokers and then open an account with one of them. Then, you have to follow certain instructions, and you will be able to buy stocks. Yes, there is definitely a ton of research involved too, and you will learn more about it in this book but what I mean to say is that the process is not too elaborate.

Even if you compare stocks with other forms of investments like investing in a business or real estate, stocks are pretty easy to deal with, and they are much faster. Moreover, you will often hear the term 'liquid assets' being used to refer to stocks, and the reason behind this is that you can turn your stocks into cash faster than any other form of investment.

Diversification

You are always advised not to stick to any one form of investment, and when you are investing your money in stocks, you are diversifying your portfolio along with your savings and CDs. This ensures that no matter how much the volatility of the market is, you will still be protected. You will see that when there is a downfall in the stock market, the bond market rises. So, if you have invested money in both, you will be gaining in one when you are losing in the other. That is why I would also advise you not to put all your eggs in one basket and invest some of your money in stocks.

Chapter 2:
Fundamentals of the Stock Market

Before we dive into the part about trading, there are some fundamental things that you should be aware of, and in this chapter, we are going to talk about those fundamentals. People often take a step back from investing in stocks because they think they are going to lose all their money if they try to do so. But if you make informed decisions after considerable research, the stock market will no longer seem so alienated.

What Is the Stock Market?

So, for those of you who are totally new to investing in the stock market, I am going to give you a basic understanding of what it is. It is basically a collection of markets that consists of shares, and there is regular issuance, buying, and selling of these shares. These shares are owned by publicly-held companies. When you buy these stocks, you basically are now the owner of a particular share of that company. The earnings of the company are what determine the price of the stocks. There are several formal exchanges through which the financial activities related to stocks take place, and they are also known as OTC or over-the-counter marketplaces. They are not allowed to perform in any way they seem fit because they are governed by a fixed set of regulations.

The basic question that every beginner has is, why do these companies sell the stocks? Now, this is because they want to grow their company and make their funds large. For example, let us say you want to start your own business, what do you do for the financing? You either use your credit card, or you apply for a personal loan, right? And then, you can also opt for loans from a bank when your company has reached a certain level. These companies are also the same. When they need money, they can first start by selling their bonds to investors they deem fit. But sooner or later, they are going to need a lot of money so that they can upgrade their business to the next level. That is when the initial public offering happens. In simpler terms, the company starts selling stocks. Now, the company is no longer the property of any single person. It has been divided into parts and every person who has bought the stocks holds some part of the company. The stock market sustains because these businesses need to raise more money for their business to grow and that is how everyone who has invested in them makes a profit.

Investing vs. Trading

Many people think that investing in stocks is the same as trading, but no, they are two completely different things. Although the ultimate aim for both these processes is to maximize your profit, they are two different entities.

If someone is trading stocks, then they are not in a particular stock for the long-term. They can jump in and out as they feel like whenever they feel they are going to make a short-term profit – it can be weeks, or it can also be minutes. They are not bothered about the prospects the company holds but rather the technical factors that are working behind the stocks. Traders are more concerned about the movement of stocks, and they try to predict these moves and also predict whether they are going to incur a profit or a loss from that move. That is how they plan their strategies.

On the contrary, investors are in the game for the long-term. No matter how much up and down the market goes through, investors usually stick through it because they are looking at the profit they are going to get in the long-term. If you are investing in the stock market and you follow the rules wisely, being a millionaire is not that much of a tough job. But yes, investors definitely need patience and enough discipline to remain in the market.

Are you confused as to what you want to be? Well, it mostly depends on how invested you want to be in the stocks market. If you want to be a trader, then you have to be prepared for spending hours in the market because you have to keep comparing graphs, check the charts, and predicting moves so that you can make a profit. But yes, no matter what you choose – be it investing or trading – you should not be investing your money in the stock market just like that without any research on a particular company.

Understand the Risk Involved

Although I am going to cover the topic of risk involved in detail in the latter part of this book, I wanted to talk about it briefly in this chapter so that you get a comprehensive idea of what the stock market is all about. Risks are always associated with any type of investment that you do. The major risk that plagues investors is an economic risk. There was a sour spell in the economy back in 2001 when there was a market bust in 2000 and the attack of 9/11. The economy definitely took years to return back to normalcy. If you are just a beginner and a young investor, I would advise you to lie low and ride out these bad phases. Also, if your domestic market is suffering, you can look to foreign stocks. But if you are nearing your retirement and suddenly the market changes its course towards the negative, then you will be in for huge losses, and that is also why I had spoken about diversification in the first chapter.

You also have to deal with market value risk. It happens when there is a collapse because of more and more investors going out of the market. This is what happened recently due to the Covid-19 pandemic. But for every risk, there are measures that you can take to minimize the impact, and you are going to learn more about it in Chapter 9.

Participants of the Stock Market

There are different types of participants in the stock market, and in this section, we are going to discuss the function of each one of them. Some of them play quite unique roles, but there are others whose roles are connected to one another. In order to allow the market to run productively, each and every one of these participants have to work in unison.

Stockbrokers

The role of buying and selling orders for different securities, including stocks, is performed by stockbrokers, and sometimes you will find them being referred to as only 'broker.' They manage the transactions of not only the institutional customers but also several retail customers, mostly through a brokerage firm. In return for the services that they are providing, the stockbrokers get their own cut known as commissions. There is no fixed rate for these commissions and the rates vary from one firm to the other. Yes, it is true that you don't have to absolutely depend on stockbrokers and you can go and buy the stocks from the company itself but in that case, you will have to take up a lot of hassle. On the other hand, buying stocks through a stockbroker makes the process so much easier to deal with.

Previously, it was not easy to approach or even afford a stockbroker mainly because they charged a hefty fee and so their use was limited only to the investors with high net-worth. But now, a lot has changed, especially because of the advances made in technology and the rapid rise of the internet. So, you now have discount brokers whose services can be availed not only much faster but also at cheaper rates compared to the previous scenario. So, investing in the stock market has now become more plausible because of the lesser transaction fees involved. Moreover, even if you are located overseas, you can invest in any particular stock market because of the presence of these discount brokers. The credentialing requirements, although are not fixed and vary from one country to another.

Portfolio Managers

The next participant that we are going to talk about is the portfolio managers who are mainly responsible for maintaining the intricacies of portfolio trading, and it can be either passive or active. No matter what the type of the fund is, it is highly influenced by the portfolio manager. The returns that come from any particular fund are also highly dependent on the portfolio manager. So, in order to become a portfolio manager, you definitely have to have a strong background in relation to finance like that of a broker, trader, or an experienced investor. The selling and buying decisions of a portfolio are made by these portfolio managers, and there are several analysts who give them these recommendations.

Investment Bankers

When it comes to raising capital for different entities like the government or other corporations, then the individual responsible for that task is an investment banker. Some of the major investment banks are Morgan Stanley, Goldman Sachs, Deutsche Bank, and JPMorgan Chase. All the complicated transactions are handled by them. In order to raise the money, they help in issuing securities. By hiring an investment banker, the company saves its time because they do not have to do any research about strategies or risks involved. Everything about the present investing climate will be assessed by the investment banker, and they can also help in understanding the various regulatory requirements. When the IPO or an initial public offering of a company is held, all the shares of that company are bought by the investment bank. The bank, here, acts as the intermediary, and when the company is going public, it acts on the company's behalf. All the shares of the company will be liquidated because the investment bank will share them in the public market.

Custodian

To make sure that the customers do not face loss or theft, their securities are held by custodians for safekeeping. The securities can be held in either physical form or even electronic form. It is usually the reputable and large firms responsible for the securities and assets since it is not about a few amount of money but sometimes even billions of dollars. But it is not only the safekeeping of assets that custodians provide, but they also offer some other services like that of transaction settlements, account administration, foreign exchange, and tax support. Based on the services that you are demanding, the fees charged will also be different. Sometimes the total value of the holdings is what determines the quarterly fees of the custodians. The custodian also has the power of limiting your account activity when the beneficiary in question is a minor.

Market Maker

The broker-dealers are known as market makers. They not only maintain an inventory of shares, but they also help in facilitating the process of trading. For any specific set of shares, the liquidity is ensured by the market makers. He/she is also responsible for the profits made in the process.

Primary and Secondary Markets

If you want to completely understand the process of trading with respect to different securities, then knowing the distinction between primary and secondary markets is of utmost importance. The creation of securities takes place in the primary market, whereas the investors trade those securities in the secondary market. When an IPO takes place, the bonds and stocks of a company are sold to the public in the primary market. The stock market is what is referred to as the secondary market. For example, the Nasdaq, the New York Stock Exchange, and so on.

Some other types of offerings that take place in a primary market are preferential allotment and private placement. When shares are not made public, and yet there are more significant investors to whom the stocks or bonds can be sold directly by the company, for example, banks and hedge funds, then that is known as a private placement. On the other hand, in the case of preferential allotment, a special price is fixed at which the stocks are given to specific investors instead of the general public, for example, mutual funds, banks, and hedge funds. But what is even more important to understand in this concept is that in the primary market, the issuer is from whom the securities are directly bough.

In the case of the secondary market, you can buy and sell stocks to other investors. But there are two more divisions of the secondary market that you should know about, and they are –

- **Auction Market** – This is the congregation of all institutions and individuals that are interested in buying or selling stocks, and then the prices of these securities are announced. These prices are also referred to as the ask and bid prices. This results in the price that is mutually agreeable by everyone.

- **Dealer Market** – But in the case of a dealer market, you do not need a central location where both parties can converge because, in this case, everything happens through electronic networks.

Important Terms Related to the Stock Market

If you have the enthusiasm to learn about the stock market, then you have to make yourself known to certain important terms. If you are not aware of the meaning of these terms, you will not be able to acquire the basic knowledge required to make a profit in the stock market. So, here are some stock market terminologies that every beginner should get acquainted with –

Stocks

Also referred to as equity, stocks give a person the ownership of a particular fraction of a company. When you buy stocks, you basically own the assets of a corporation by a certain percentage, and the profits generated by that percentage of assets are going to be yours. Shares are basically referred to as the unit of stocks.

Common Stocks

Usually, there is only one kind of stock representing a particular company, but in certain cases, you will notice that multiple stocks are used to represent a company, and thus, that company has dual classes of stock. And the voting rights for one class of stock are usually higher than the other. If you own common stocks, then the earnings of that company will be distributed to the common stockholders proportionately. Sometimes, the profits are also distributed in the form of cash dividends.

Preferred Stocks

If a larger divided is what you want, then you should go after the preferred stocks of a company. But you are not going to get any voting rights if you hold preferred stocks. On the other hand, in case there is an insolvency approaching, you will definitely get some special status. You are on top of the hierarchy, for example, if the situation arises that all the creditors have to be paid because of the liquidation of the assets of a company, then the preferred stockholders are the ones that are going to be paid before and then the common stockholders. You cannot convert your common stock into preferred stock, but the opposite is possible.

Bonds

If I have to explain bonds to you in a very simple way, then I would say that it is like a loan. When people buy bonds, there are basically helping a company or the government out by lending them money. A future day is fixed by when the issuer of the bond will pay you back the money, and they will also be paying you certain interest in the meantime. There are corporate bonds, and then there are government bonds. There are investment-grade bonds and savings bonds as well. And then there are bond funds for those who are not confident enough to invest in the bonds directly.

Mutual Funds

As I had mentioned before, a portfolio manager is responsible for handling the workings of a mutual fund. It is nothing but a pooled portfolio, and if someone is willing to expand their exposure to a variety of bonds and stocks, then mutual funds are a great way to do so. You do not have to do any of the research work because that is what the portfolio manager is for. The trading of mutual funds does not occur all throughout the day. The values depend on the final calculated value after the entire day throughout which buy and sell orders are placed.

Exchange-Traded Funds or ETFs

They have a similar nature to that of mutual funds, and thus people often get confused between the two, but in the case of ETFs, trading occurs throughout the day. In certain cases, you can also avail of some tax advantages. Even though they are involved in the commodity market investment, ETFs are popular for keeping track of the stock indices.

Stock Market Index

The changes happening in the stock market are measured by stock market indices. At first, all the securities listed on a stock exchange are evaluated, and then similar stocks are chosen and grouped. There are different types of selection criteria for these stocks, for example, the size of the company, market capitalization, and so on. The underlying stocks have certain values assigned to them, and that value is used in finding out the value of the stock market index. For example, the index will rise when there is an overall rise in the value of the stocks and vice-versa. Thus, the price movements, as well as the market sentiments, can be measured with the help of the stock market index. So, in simpler terms, you can compare the stock market index to that of a barometer. Moreover, it makes stock-picking a much easier task by acting as a benchmark.

Bull and Bear Markets

You will see these terms being used very often throughout this book and even when you are doing some research about the stock market on your own. When the prices are either expected to rise or are rising, the condition of the market is referred to as the bull market. For example, when the prices of stocks have risen by 20%, it is called a bull market, but these situations are very difficult to actually notice, and so, most often, analysts realize a bull market only after it has happened.

On the other hand, when the prices of stocks are declining, it is referred to as the bear market. It is during this time that the rate of unemployment starts rising and the economy starts falling down gradually.

Chapter 3:
A STEP-BY-STEP GUIDE TO START INVESTING IN STOCKS

If this is your first time investing in the stock market, then I must say that it can be intimidating to start, especially because it is something totally new to you. But with proper guidance and sufficient knowledge, you will realize that it is not that difficult after all. You are often advised to invest in the stock market as early in your life as possible, mainly because of the compounding effect of stocks, which enables you to earn more money over the long term. So, in order to help you kick start your journey in the world of stocks, I have prepared a comprehensive guide for you that will show you the right path in a step-by-step manner.

Step 1 – Determine What Your Goals Are

Stock investing is not any one-lane road. There are multiple ways in which you can approach it, and if you want to know which of these approaches will be the best for you, then you have to start by determining the goals that you have. Another thing that you have to assess is your current financial status and whether you can afford to invest in stocks right now or not. And for that, you have to consider everything starting from your monthly household budget to all the debt that you owe. Here are some specific things that you should consider before diving into stock investing –

- Your employment is of a big concern here, especially because you cannot begin your journey without a proper inflow of cash. You have to ensure that you have a stable income and job so that investing in the stock market doesn't mess with your day-to-day financial needs.

- Some people have a huge outstanding credit that they have to pay back and yet they choose to invest in stocks. That is not right. If you are someone with a significant amount of debt that you still owe, you have to deal with that first. Investing in the stock market is really good, but you should not pour in the money that you would need in your own life; in simpler terms, don't buy stocks with money you cannot afford to lose.

- You should also consider your present family situation. Have you just had a baby, or have you moved to a completely different city? If so, then you are going to have a lot of finances to deal with, and so, your income has to remain steady. You cannot afford any losses. That is why you should consider deferring stock market investment to a time when you will become completely settled.

- Lastly, think about your monthly household budget and decide whether you can really keep some cash aside for stock market investments.

Once you have figured these out, the next thing that you have to think about is your goal. You have to figure out the 'why' behind your investment venture. Ask yourself, what do you want the extra income for? Is it for your retirement, or do you have something in mind for about five-eight years down the lane? When you figure out the 'why' shaping your decisions will become way easier. And in order to make these decisions, you do not really have to know anything about the stock market because these decisions are more about your personal life. If you are finding it difficult to figure out your goals, then take a piece of paper and write down all that you want to have in your life from a financial point of view and then start assigning a time to each one of them – a particular within which you want to achieve those things. Then, you have to judge the urgency and importance of your goals and invest accordingly.

But, in general, stock market investments are usually more profitable when you do them for the long-term. In case you are investing them in the short-term, the risk factor will become high, and you might lose some money.

Step 2 – Educate Yourself About the Stock Market

Once you are done with the first step, it is time that you start familiarizing yourself with the basics of the stock market. You have to learn how everything works and what are the essential components of investing in stocks?

One of the most important things that you should do a bit of research about is the different stock exchanges. Then, get to know the terminologies used in the market. I have listed some basic ones in the previous chapter, and you will find more in the chapters to come. The next most important thing to learn is stock valuation. For this, you have to dig into the fundamental analysis. Then, try to know about the various types of securities involved and also learn the advantages and disadvantages of all of them.

If you want your portfolio to look good, one of the most important things to learn is stock valuation. Also, you have to understand that you cannot separate the risk factor from the stock market. The risk will always be there, but what you have to do is understand how much risk you are ready to tolerate or rather you can afford to tolerate. That is why your risk tolerance should be in line with your goals if you want to do stock investing in the right way.

Step 3 – Always Have a Cash Reserve

This is such an important step, and most people overlook it before investing in the stock market. A cash reserve is something that everyone should have. This reserve will have some money that you will put away for yourself so that no matter the risk, you always have some money in your hand. And this cash reserve should not be kept in any risky investment. I would advise you to keep it in money market accounts or certificates of deposit.

Now, you must be thinking about what the actual function of this cash reserve is. Well, for starters, it will act as the emergency fund so that in case you have to face a financial emergency or any type of temporary income disruption, you have a handsome amount of money in your hand. The second reason for having a cash reserve is that even if your investments take a sudden wrong turn, you do not have to panic.

Step 4 – Start By Opening a Retirement Account

So, after you have your cash reserve ready, the next thing that you should do is open a retirement account. If you want to get it through your employer, then a 401 (k) plan is what you should go for. Otherwise, you can also choose an IRA or Individual Retirement Plan, which is a very popular one among people who are self-employed or are freelancers.

One of the best methods of long-term investing is

these retirement accounts. They can save tax, and in most cases, payroll deductions are what keeps them running. Your money will keep growing silently over the years, and when you retire, you don't have to think about how you are going to spend the rest of the years. The best thing about these accounts is that you can allow the money to keep accumulating in the plan until you decide to bring in the funds and stocks.

Step 5 – Choose a Low-Cost Online Service

After setting up your retirement account, the next thing that I will advise you to do is start looking out for your non-retirement needs.

There are two options from which you can choose, and I am going to explain both of them in this section –

- **Robo Advisor** – The first option is choosing a robo advisor, and these are basically responsible for building you an ideal portfolio having the right mix of everything to balance your risk exposure and specific algorithms are used to create this portfolio. You will not be able to choose the funds or stocks on your own because everything is done by the robo advisor. Do some research online about which robo advisor suits you best. Some of them do not even require any amount of initial investment. Keep using the robo advisor until you are ready to invest in stocks yourself.

- **Online Stock Broker** – Once you think you are ready to embrace the market fully, you have to choose an online stockbroker. With them, you will be doing everything on your own starting from choosing your stocks to even making the buying and selling decisions. There are several things to keep in mind before you choose your online stockbroker, and we are going to discuss them in the latter part of this book.

Step 6 – Start By Investing in ETFs or Mutual Funds

I have always advised beginners not to dive into direct stock, investing right away. You need to get well-acquainted with the market before you make such decisions. That is why you should start with ETFs or mutual funds. The main reason behind this is because mutual funds or even ETFs are managed by professionals who are experts in this field. You don't have to deal with the strenuous and extensive work of selecting stocks, and that will be done by the portfolio managers. The only thing that you have to decide is to figure out how much you want to invest in any particular fund. You can also invest in a group of funds. But once you have figured out the investment amount, your work is basically over. The rest of the decisions will be made by the fund managers.

Another burden that is taken off from your shoulders in the case of mutual funds is that you don't have to worry about diversifying your portfolio. There are different types of stocks present in each of these portfolios, and thus, every fund has already been diversified. Also, if you compare with the commissions charged for investing directly in stocks, mutual funds have a benefit because the fees remain the same as long as you meet with all the requirements. You can invest as low as $50, and so, almost everyone can invest their money in mutual funds.

Step 7 – Stick With Index Funds

Before I tell you why you should stick with index funds, let me give you a brief intro of what index funds are. These are nothing, but mutual funds or ETFs but the securities that are present under index funds are all on a specific index. The ultimate goal of these securities is that they should become as close to the benchmark as possible. One of the most popular and important indexes that are followed is the S&P 500.

In the previous step, I told you to start investing with mutual funds, but in case you want the process to be even more hassle-free, then invest in index funds. The main benefit is that when you are investing in index funds, your fund is never going to underperform but at the same time, they are not going to over-perform either. So, basically, this is the safest bet for everyone and especially for a new investor. If you see the records from previous years, you will see that the total return in the case of index funds has always been greater than other types of funds. Moreover, since index funds are managed passively, their management fees are also much lower compared to others.

Step 8 – Use Dollar-Cost Averaging

This is basically a special type of strategy with the help of which you can reduce the impact of volatility on your portfolio. If you understand the process, then your portfolio can benefit highly from this strategy. In this process, instead of investing a huge amount of money and buying a lot of stocks at a time, you are going to buy them gradually over a certain period of time. What I mean to say is that in the case of dollar-cost averaging, you are going to invest your money, say $100 every month, instead of investing $4000 in a single fund. But do you know why you are doing this? The primary reason is to avoid the chances of buying at the top of the market.

When you are making gradual purchases, you are basically buying into the fund continuously but at different times. You do not have to think about when is the best time to invest in a fund if you are doing dollar-cost averaging. One of the major benefits of adopting this strategy is that you will not be swayed by your emotions into investing a huge chunk of money and so you will be saving yourself from any kind of psychological biases whatsoever. Greed and fear are two things that can completely destroy your stock investment strategies, but with dollar-cost averaging, you are able to beat any such tendencies.

Step 9 – Slowly Start Investing in Individual Stocks

After you have completed all of the above steps, you will start feeling comfortable with the entire investment procedure. But you have to do it gradually; otherwise, it is quite easy to face an overwhelming situation. Another thing that you have to keep in mind is that if you take the decision of investing in individual stocks, then you can no longer use the strategy of dollar-cost averaging. Once you have made your significant share of investments in ETFs and mutual funds, take your time to build your portfolio. You should not increase your exposure to any particular stock. Any one stock should not hold more than 10% of your portfolio.

Also, as a beginner, I would advise you not to take a huge position in any stock. If you want the pricing to be on your side and, at the same time not overload on the stock, 100 shares should be a good place to start. After that, invest in some other stock and keep doing this same process until your portfolio has been filled with several stocks apart from the previous ETFs and mutual funds.

Step 10 – Always Diversify

If you are investing in the stock market, diversification is the key to reducing risks. This is because when you invest in a variety of assets, any single asset will not be able to affect you. For example, if any single asset performs badly, you always have something else to cover for you. If you have followed every single step that I have mentioned above, then your portfolio has already been diversified to a great extent, and when you finally start to invest in individual stocks, you are diversifying your portfolio even more. But there is another thing to keep in mind, and that is – you should select different types of equity sectors to spread your capital.

Some factors that need to considered before diversification is your age and your risk appetite. But in general, you should spread your capital in income funds, growth funds, bonds, and international funds. There should be a proper balance between your income holdings and your growth assets. One of the major reasons I advised you to invest in ETFs and mutual funds is because of diversification. Having them in your portfolio ensures that it is already diversified to a certain extent.

Chapter 4:
CAN YOU INVEST IN STOCKS WITH A LOW INVESTMENT?

Are you worried about the fact that you have too little money to invest in stocks? Well, if you ask me, in today's world, no amount of money is too little to invest in stocks, and this is mainly because there is no minimum amount as to how much you can invest. Also, it is better to invest something than investing nothing. If you want to increase your wealth over time, you have to learn the art of saving your money. This doesn't happen in one day and it usually involves you putting away some money every day in order to develop good habits. If you are going to Starbucks every day for your daily cuppa, swap it for homemade coffee, and you are going to save at least $50 there. In this chapter, I am going to show how it's possible to invest in stocks with a very small amount of investment as well.

Invest Your Spare Change

If you haven't heard about the spare change apps, then I am going to explain them here in this section. The younger generations are using these apps a lot these days, and these apps are truly good for beginner investors. The millennial generation is not investing enough, and the spare change apps can really change the dynamics of investment. In fact, did you know that 40% of millennials do not have any investment because they think that they do not have enough money for it? If you ask people around you, most of them will tell you that they didn't enter the stock market because it takes a lot of money to start. But investing in today's world has become really simple and there are several ways in which you can start with a small investment.

You can start by investing even just a few dollars with the help of certain spare change apps. Some of the most commonly used ones are Acorns, Stash, and Clink. It is true that these apps are not for anyone, but if you are someone not investing with the excuse that you do not have enough money, then these apps are perfect, to begin with. Even if you have $5, you can start investing with these apps. In fact, cutting off certain daily luxuries will help you save up for investing with the help of these apps. There is another added benefit of using these apps, and that is, if your total amount is below $5000, then you simply have to pay a fee of $1 in a month and that's it. That is why these apps are perfect for beginners. Moreover, they have been designed in an extremely user-friendly way so tracking your progress or even setting up your account does not involve any such hassle at all.

But no matter what app you are using, you should always dig a bit deeper and see if there are any hidden costs involved. Sometimes, you might be paying low fees monthly, but then that fees depend on how much you are saving. If your savings go beyond the limit, then you might have to pay a fee of as much as 10% of the saved amount. And if the situation is that, then you will be paying much lower fees with online brokers, but with them, the minimum balance required is much more.

You will usually be introduced to different types of portfolio options when you open an account with one of these micro-investing apps. You have to select the type of portfolio you want to build. Some of them will also ask you to answer a few questions on how you want to use the account and whether you want to be able to withdraw the money any time you want. At a certain point in time, you will be asked to connect your bank account, and after that, you can even choose the option of automatic payments. These automatic payments can be either made monthly or weekly. If you indeed choose to set the automatic payments, you first have to look at your monthly budget and decide whether you are sure to have that money ready by the end of each month.

Use an Online Broker

An online broker can help you invest in the stock market, even when your investment is small. In the next chapter, I am going to give you a step-by-step guide on how to choose the right broker, but here, in this section, you will learn how an online broker is beneficial for those who want to step into the stock market but with a low investment.

There are different online brokers available. You should compare the fees and costs of each one of them because some of them can really offer low fees. You will get all this information on the interface that the broker has. If you are going to invest through your phone, make sure the broker has an app.

If you have a limited investment amount that is

small, the first thing that you should check is the minimum deposit requirement of the broker. But don't worry as there are several brokers who have really low minimum requirements. In fact, even if you are not ready to give an initial deposit, some of them will still allow you to open an account with them. These are usually called the zero balance accounts. All you have to do is a little bit of research, and you will get to know all of this. Sometimes, the minimum requirement is waived off on fulfilling certain criteria, so you should be looking out for such things as well.

Once you have got the broker of your choice, you need to set up an account. It is very similar to setting up your bank account. You will probably need only a few minutes to set up your account. After you are done with the basics, the first thing that you will have to do is link your bank account. And then, you can make your first transfer. In order to buy the stocks or the money to be available in your account, you might have to wait for a couple of days. But use this waiting time to learn more about the stock market and research about different strategies. There is literally so much to learn if you want to.

If you are someone with a fixed income and you are

determined about investing regularly, then I think you should set automatic transfers of small amounts. But if you are not that confident or if your income keeps varying, especially if you are a freelancer, then you can also make individual payments towards your account whenever you have the monetary capacity to do so.

One of the major benefits of opening an account with an online broker is that you will get access to their tools and research material that will help you know more details about stocks and perform your own analysis about the market. In fact, some of the brokers also have instructional and guidance material on how you can choose stocks or market trends, and so on. So, you should check these out as well. One of the first things that you should check is the history and performance of the company that you are thinking about investing in, and some brokers can produce almost 5-10 years of data to study. When you have saved a considerable amount of money, you can then go for the full-service brokers because they offer an even wider range of services with more tools and resources.

Like I already told you in the previous chapter, you need to have a diversified portfolio, and so, you need to choose multiple stocks to invest in. Even if you have a small investment amount, you should be dividing that amount into two companies. And while choosing these companies, make sure you have checked their history of profitability and stability.

Here is one small tip that I can give you – look for stocks that belong to good companies but now are in the downtrend. Every company goes through an off phase, but there will come a point when they see an upward rise, and that is when you are going to earn a good profit.

Once your account has accumulated a good amount of cash, you should do another round of stock picking and invest, and in the same way, you should gradually increase your investments. Like this, grow your portfolio to about five to six stocks.

Invest in a Retirement Plan Sponsored By Your Employer

Retirement plans are a very good option to invest in if you do not have a higher initial investment amount, but first, you have to find out what retirement plans are provided by your employer. It is quite natural for you to know it already because the orientations are where such information is already given, but in case you don't know it or you don't seem to remember it, you should find it out. Also, in certain cases, you will become eligible for these retirement plans only when you have worked for a certain period of time, say 90 days. You can also take the employee handbook and see whether you can find any information there. If you don't get anything, then it's best that you ask someone from the HR department or your manager.

Usually, both Roth 401(k) and traditional 401(k) plans are provided, but you have to understand the difference between the two. If you are choosing the former, then all your contributions towards it will be deducted from your income after adjusting the taxes, whereas, in the case of the latter, the contributions will be deducted from your income but pre-tax. Again, if you need more information, someone from the HR department would definitely be able to answer your queries.

When you are interested in these retirement plans, and you let your office know about it, you will most likely be put in touch with someone handling such stuff, for example, a plan administrator. After that, you will be introduced to the different types of investment options open to you. But if you want some more information, you can get in touch with a financial advisor of your own too.

Now, if you are young, then you probably do not have much to save after adjusting all your daily expenses from your salary. So, what you should do is that start small. I would suggest that you should be able to input at least 1 or 2 percent of your salary towards the retirement plan. Also, you have to make a promise to yourself that when you get a pay raise, you are going to increase your investment towards your retirement plan as well. In this way, you can ensure that your investments keep on increasing with time. So, if you are contributing about 3 percent now, then you should try to increase that by about 2 percent after a pay raise.

So, now that you have read all the three ways in which you can invest in stocks, even if you have a low investment amount, let me tell you something. The trick is to invest smartly. If you want to be a successful investor in your life, you don't necessarily have to invest big bucks, but you do need to make some smart decisions. Also, if you have debts in your hand, you should end them first. Also, when you get your tax refund, make sure you keep some of that money in your hand so that you can invest it in the stocks. And lastly, look for any way in which you can reduce the investment fees and that is why you need to choose your broker wisely. We are going to discuss more of it in the next chapter.

Chapter 5:

TIPS TO CHOOSE THE RIGHT BROKER

If you want your investments to reap a good amount of profit, you have to make a smart choice regarding the brokerage service that you are using. The online brokers are not all the same. The features differ from one broker to another. You should consider both your education needs and your investing goals before you settle for a particular online broker. Also, if you are a new investor, then you have to be even more careful because all of this is new for new, and you are excited to try out this new endeavor, but once you have made a bad decision, all of this can quickly become a nightmare.

It is true that nothing can actually guarantee you a good and handsome return, but yes, it is entirely in your own hands as to whether you are setting yourself up for success or not. In this chapter, I am going to provide you with a comprehensive guide on how you can choose the right brokerage for yourself.

Understand Your Needs

If you are already searching for these things on the internet, then the chances are that you have come across plenty of brokerage ads by now, but before you click on any of them, you have to start figuring out what is it that you are really searching for in a broker. The answer will differ from one person to another and will mostly depend on the investment goals that you have. But start by being honest with yourself and see where you are on the learning curve. If you are someone who has started out a few days back, then you are probably not even aware of all the basics. In that case, what you should prioritize are comprehensive glossaries that will give you the meaning of every possible term that comes your way, educational resources explaining all the basics, access to data from previous years, and a friendly support staff that can be reached at any time.

If you have already grasped the basic or fundamental concepts, then you should look for brokers that can provide you with technical and fundamental analysis data and education on the stock market but something of a higher level. But in order to do all of this, you have to be completely honest with yourself; otherwise, this is not going to work out. Also, you need to ask yourself whether you are more interested in passive investments, or you want to set up a retirement account. Do you want a professional overseeing everything for you or do you want to do it all by yourself? These were only some of the questions and there are many more that you should ask yourself and it will vary from one person to another. If your answers are changing over the course of time, don't worry, it happens to everyone. You only have to focus on what you have now and you can deal with the rest when it comes.

Narrow Down the Options

Once you have clearly visualized your needs, it is time you start narrowing down the playing field because there will be multiple brokers at your disposal, and you have to settle with one. Here are some of the points that will help you in narrowing down your options –

- Check whether the disclaimer says that the online broker is a member of SIPC or not. SIPC stands for Securities Investor Protection Corporation. You can also visit the website of SIPC to find out.

- Another point to look for is whether the broker is a member of FINRA. It should not be too difficult to find because these things are usually stated in quite obvious places for the people to see. FINRA stands for Financial Industry Regulatory Authority.

- Don't forget to check the type of insurance that the brokerage is providing. When a brokerage firm is a member of SIPC, they are mandatorily required to provide insurance to everyone in case the company fails.

- Also, in the case, someone experiences fraud, will the company be providing any kind of protection? Sometimes, you have to meet a lot of criteria in order to be reimbursed. Make sure you check those too. In case you have to maintain certain precautions to be reimbursed, don't forget to check them as well.

- In today's world, you can check the reviews of almost anything online, and brokerage firms are no different. Google the companies and see what other customers have to say about them. You can also use keywords like customer service, fraud protection, and insurance claim. But yes, don't believe just about anything you see because in certain cases, we all know that not all reviews are true. But if you see a similar bad review cropping up everything, then you should definitely look deeper into it.

- You should check whether the website of the broker is using cookies or encryption, and you can even query about the methods or steps that the broker is using to ensure your account is safe.

- All the brokers will offer you standard accounts that are taxable. But you should research whether any of them is providing something else or not. Some brokers offer custodial accounts that you can use in the case of a minor, and some offer ESA or Education Savings Account.

- Another thing that you should definitely check is whether there is a minimum amount of investment for all of these accounts. You should also ask whether you can open a retirement account or not.

Enquire About the Fees

After you have gathered all the information that I have mentioned above, you probably have a lot of information in your hand to narrow down your options, but there is another important thing that you should check, and that is the fee that the online broker is going to charge. You should never be doing business with any online broker until and unless you have a clear idea of what their fees are. Your ultimate aim should be not to lose most of your returns to these brokerage fees. But at times, the premium that is charged by the online brokers becomes justifiable based on the fact that they are offering way more than their competitors who are relatively cheaper.

The first thing to check is whether they have a deposit minimum or not, and if they have, then how much is that? Sometimes, online brokers charge maintenance fees either monthly or annually. You should find out about these too and in certain cases, the company agrees to waive off these fees when you have a larger account. Sometimes, the option to waive off such fees is related to other conditions as well.

Some of the brokers also have an advanced platform

for those who will agree to pay them a higher amount of money. These advanced platforms mostly have tools and resources that you will need to take your investing game to the next level. In some cases, brokers offer their advanced services for free, but only when the customer has made a certain minimum investment or trades in a year.

The next thing that you have to figure out is the trading commissions. Sometimes these commissions differ with the size of your account. In other cases, the commissions differ with the type of securities you are dealing with. Some brokers also offer advisory services, but they are usually chargeable. Whether you are going to use them now or not, it is always better to know about them so that you can use them in the future when you have the money to afford them.

Test the Platform

Once you have selected a couple of online brokers, it is time you test their platforms to make your final choice. Usually, you will get a comprehensive description of all the resources and tools that are broker has, but nothing can replace the experience you will get in a test drive. Sometimes, you will get companies that will offer you to open an account for free, and so, I would advise you to sign-up on their website. In this way, you will get access to certain parts of the trading platform and see how it works.

Look for all the metrics they are providing and whether they are meeting your expectations or not. In some platforms, they even offer you settings where you can set up alerts whenever there is a matching pattern. See, if the broker is offering any such features or not. You should also check things like whether the broker is allowing you to make any notes that you can use for future references, like maintaining an online journal on their website.

You should visit the website at various timings throughout the day because you definitely do not want to open an account with a broker who has a slow website. Finance is all about timing, and a website lagging in speed can be your worst enemy in the stock market. No matter what type of investor or trader you are, never settle for a broker with a slow website.

Check the Reliability of the Customer Service

Never settle on the words of the online broker when it comes to customer service. You have to check it for yourself to see whether they are really what you expected or not. You should definitely prioritize reliable customer support. Moreover, this point is even more important for anyone new to the world of stocks. There might be times when you need the help of the customer support, and if they are not there to help you out, you will be blindsided.

Start by thinking, what are the types of contact that you prefer? Do you want an email that you can get a reply from at any time, or do you want a phone number? You can also ask about live chat support since those are so popular nowadays. Ask whether their technical support is available at all times all throughout the year or whether it is available only on weekdays. Some brokers even have options where they will set you up with representatives who will be responsible for answering questions about your account only and so you should enquire whether the broker is going to provide you with any such service or not.

All the questions you have should be clarified before you finalize a platform, and so, you should reach out to their customer service and see whether they are willing to answer your questions or how much time they are taking to cater to your queries.

The Online Broker Platform Should Be User-Friendly

Whether you are going to be trading or investing, the platform must be user-friendly. Sometimes the brokers have different platforms for beginners and advanced stock market traders and investors. Some of them offer full mobile functionality, while some will provide you with only partial mobile functionality. These are some of the things that you should try to know about. All of this can be easily found out when you are testing the platform. See whether you literally have to hunt for the information you are searching for or whether everything is within your reach. Is it easy to invest in stocks and place a trade, or is there a huge and complex process involved?

If you still cannot figure out these things, many of the platforms offer guided platform tours, and you should look for them. Usually, they can be found on the website itself but in case you cannot find them, make a query. You should also look for any type of video tutorials or screenshots that will tell you about the different functions of the platform. Some of the brokers even offer simulated trading platforms and you should take full advantage of these if you are planning to go into trading. Also, you should check whether you will be getting things like a quotes feed that is frequently updated, screening tools, or risk detectors. Also, keep in mind that sometimes such fancy stuff can cost extra bucks, and you should look for any such fees involved before making any final decisions.

Lastly, remember that price is not the only criterion that should dictate your choice. You have to make a comparison of all the features that you are getting and then settle for the one that you find the best.

Chapter 6:

HOW TO EARN REGULAR INCOME THROUGH STOCK MARKET INVESTING?

If you are investing in the stock market and anticipating a regular income from it, then I would advise you to invest in dividend stocks. But before that, you should have a proper idea of what dividend stocks are.

One of the most direct ways in which the profits of a company can be distributed among the shareholders is dividends. Also, if you have invested in a company that is reliable and if the stocks are in a good state, then you definitely have the potential to earn handsome profits on a regular basis form the dividend stocks. This is also one of the major reasons why they are so much popular among retirees. On investing in these stocks, you can ensure that your cash stream remains constant. Moreover, when compared to the growth stocks, the volatility of the dividend stocks are way lesser. That's why they are also helpful in minimizing the risk in your portfolio and diversifying it.

If you are not sure how you can start investing in dividend stocks, then you are in the right place, because in this chapter, I am going to show you exactly that.

Research Quality Stocks

Dividend investing is one of the most stable methods of investing in the stock market, and although the growth is slow, it is steady. Moreover, you will be protected against inflation. But researching your stocks is the most important step of dividend investing; otherwise, everything can quickly escalate in the wrong direction.

One of the first things that you should look for is that the company whose stocks you are investing in should have a consistent profit history. If you notice that there are no steady profits in the company's list, you should not consider investing in it. Your parameters of choosing stocks have to be tightened so that you can settle for the best. The growth expectations of the long-term earnings should be anywhere from 5-15%. There are companies with rates of more than 15% but try to avoid going for them; otherwise, you might have to face certain disappointments. But profit can only be maintained when the cash flow of a company is sufficient. That is why you should choose companies whose dividend has seen considerable growth in the period of the past five years or so. This will increase the likelihood of consistent dividend growth in the coming years as well. You can also maintain a margin of safety, and for that, you have to follow the payout ratio. You can find this out by using the net earnings to divide the dividends. The value of this ratio should be below 40%. But in the case of REITs, utilities, or MLPs, this payout ratio cannot be applied.

If the values of return-on-equity or RoE are not directly mentioned, you can calculate it yourself. Check the income statement for the net income. Then, divide the value by shareholder's equity (you will get this value by subtracting liabilities from assets, and you can get this on the balance sheet). These values should be at least 15%. If you get 20% or more, then it is even better.

You should steer clear of those companies that have excessive debt in their name. If you are unsure of the amount of debt a company owes, you should have a look at its debt-to-equity ratio. If you find that this ratio is high, it is your cue to look for your company somewhere else. Ideally, if the ratio is anywhere north of 2.0, you should not consider that company on your list. Also, you can stay at peace if the ratio is less than 1.0.

Here is another thing that you should keep a check on – uninterrupted dividend payments. If you get data of the past twenty years, then have a look at it; otherwise, you should check for at least the past ten years. The website of the company usually has this information. One more thing to note is whether the dividends are showing a gradual increase over the course of the years. Even if the divided did not see an increase every year, you have to ensure that there was an increase at least every two years or so. If the stocks that you are seeing are not meeting any of these criteria, then you should be rejecting it from your list then and there. There is no use in setting yourself up for disappointment.

But the history of a stock is not the only aspect that should be checked. Things keep changing based on market conditions too. For example, if more and more customers become health-conscious, then all the soft-drinks companies are going to suffer no matter how much profit they have made in the earlier years. After considering all the factors that I have mentioned in this section, your task will be to make a list of all the probable companies that you might be interested in. You can also consider companies from your daily life that are renowned and stable and also show a healthy record in the case of profits. To make this process easier, you can also use online stock screeners.

Look At the Stock's Quote

The stock quote is going to tell you a lot more about the dividends paid by a stock. Basically, with the help of this stock quote, you will get an idea of the price of the stock as per the price quoted on the exchange. Some other information included in this quote is the trading volume, ask and bid price, and yield too. The best financial and stock-based news are found on Yahoo Finance, Google Finance, and so on, and any latest stock quotes can also be found there for free.

Go to the label of annualized dividends or divided and look at the information mentioned there. The information that you see in this section is basically a measure from last year as to how much money for every share was paid out by the company to the investors. In case you do not find this information, it most probably means that the profit-sharing option for that stock is not available to investors at the moment.

Purchase the Stock

Your next step should be to purchase the stock. Once you are sure that you have finally found the stock that fits all the criteria, it is time that you purchase it. You can do so either directly from the company or through a broker. There are certain companies that give the chance of direct purchase, but for that, you have to do a little bit of research as to which companies have that option. But there is something that you should be aware of in this respect – you might have to pay a sum of about $25 to $500 as a minimum investment when you want to purchase the stock directly. This will obviously vary with the individual share's price and the policies of the corporation.

If there is no such option of direct purchase for the stock that you want or the minimum investment is something you don't want to do, then the option left with you is to approach the brokerage. The purchases will be facilitated by them, and you don't have to worry about anything. If you search online, you will know that there are several such brokerage firms who can help you out in this respect, and they are all operating online. The fees, commissions, minimum account balances, and other features keep differing and if you go to Chapter 5, you will see that I have already explained the process of choosing a broker in detail.

So, after you have opened your account and you are all set up, it is time for you to request a buy, and you can either do this through the mobile platform or even through the website. The transaction will be facilitated by the broker, and once it's done and you have got the stocks, you will basically become the owner of the part of the corporation that those stocks represent.

Keep Track of Your Dividends

Do you know that the companies do not have any obligation when it comes to paying the shareholders dividends? Yes, the company has the freedom to eliminate, lower, or even raise the dividends whenever they want, and so this makes it even more important for you to keep track of the dividends because if you don't, then who will? You can use your brokerage account for this task. In case you notice that the dividends have fallen to some threshold level that you had set and this is much lower than your needs, then you should consider selling those stocks.

In this respect, I would also love to inform you about the two options that are present in your hand when it comes to the collection of dividends – the first one is quite obvious, and that is a direct cash payment whereas the second one is that you can use the dividend reinvestment plan or DRIP of the company for reinvesting the dividend in that same company. I know what you must be thinking that how is this second method going to benefit you. Well, when you are reinvesting your dividends, you are doing so in more shares, and this happens on payday. For this, you have to contact your broker. But if you don't want to avail of the DRIP, then you can use your brokerage account to deposit your dividends in your savings or checking account.

Manage Your Investment Funds

The last that I am going to explain to you in order to help you earn a regular income from dividends is giving you a few tips on how you can manage your investment funds.

The first thing to keep in mind is that you have to reduce your spending and it should be quite lesser than what you are earning. You have to pay yourself first. What I mean to say is that when you get money from dividends, use a portion of it to support yourself. You should focus on investing your money, but that investment should not be more than what you are earning; otherwise, that is going to pose a problem. So, you have to plan your returns in such a way that they come back more every year, and you have enough money to not only reinvest in stocks but also invest in yourself. Let us say that you have earned $2500 in a year simply from dividends. So, from that amount, you should not spend more than $2200 on buying new stocks.

Now, let's talk about keeping aside some money. When you are earning a regular income through dividends, you should also keep in mind to keep some of it aside for money market funds or even to meet your regular living expenses. So, some of it also has to be kept in cash. I am not saying this just for your emergency fund. Sometimes, you will go through ups and downs in your time at the stock market, and when you have some extra money on the side, it will help you smooth out the curves. In case the investments did not give you sufficient returns for the upcoming month or two, you know that you always have this extra money on the side that will help you sustain. Let us say that you have calculated your yearly living expenses to be $60,000, and this does not include the funds for stock trading. You should always have an equal amount of money available either in a money market account with higher interest or in the bank. So, basically, you should keep another $60,000 somewhere that is easily accessible. This will ensure that you have a year's worth of expenses piled up.

After you have accumulated your one year's worth of expenses, it is time that you use the excess money in your hand towards investments. But you always have to keep tracking your expenses so that you can have the next year's expenses ready in hand. If the amount of money in the bank or money market accounts has amounted to so much that can sustain yourself for the next fifteen months, then you have to reduce it to twelve months and then use the extra money for making more investments. You should also set up a retirement account like I told you before in this book.

You should also maintain an Excel spreadsheet where you will be keeping track of all the purchases that you are making in the stock market. You can also record the dividend yields, stock prices, and any other piece of information that you think would be helpful in your planning process.

Then, the next thing that you have to do in order to maintain this steady flow of income is that you have to prepare a monthly cash flow budget. In this, you will mention your projected revenue from dividends, all your expenses, and other things. Once everything has been noted down, you have to check whether the revenue that you are getting is sufficient to cover for the expenses. You also have to check how much profit you are making so that you can figure out how much you can reinvest.

Are you enjoying this book? it is important to me, I would be very happy if you leave me a short review on Amazon! Thanks you.

Chapter 7:
AN INTRODUCTION TO DAY TRADING AND SWING TRADING

In this book, I am going to discuss briefly both day trading and swing trading although if you want to know more about them, you should check out my next books, which have detailed information on these trading styles. If you have been in the stock market, then you already know about these two terms – day trading and swing trading. But do you know what they mean? If not, then don't worry because we are going to discuss exactly that in this chapter. The one similarity between both is that they are all about short-term profits from trading and making the best out of small movements, but there are a lot of things that hugely different between both these trading practices.

Who Is a Day Trader?

As you might have understood from the term, day trading is when you trade every day, and so it is an active form of trading. You have to buy a security and then sell it on the same day in order to become a day trader. The stock markets and the foreign exchange markets are the places where this type of trading is more common. Day traders are usually well-funded and well-educated. They utilize a lot of short-term trading strategies, and they also have lots of leverage. They put all their focus on the small price movements that happen in the market. Anything that can place an impact on the market expectations like interest rates, corporate announcement, or any type of economic statistics are what influences the small price movements and so a day trader has to be wary about them. In the initial months as a day trader, people often end up losing huge amounts of money because of one thing, and that is – they are not well-accustomed to this method of trading. But eventually, everyone figures out a strategy that works well for them.

What Is Swing Trading?

Now that you know what day trading is, let us see what swing trading is all about. In the case of swing trading, you will be looking into any kind of swings or changes in the currencies, commodities, and shares of the market. In the case of swing trading, you can hold your assets a bit longer than day trading, say about a few days or weeks because the trades in swing trading sometimes take a bit time to work out. If you have been in the market even for a couple of months, you will know that the market goes through certain periods of trends where there are ups and downs in prices, and these trends are exactly what you have to track in the case of swing trading. Several technical indicators are used for this, and you will learn in detail about them in my next books.

Day Trading vs. Swing Trading

The profitability and trading strategy can be hugely affected by the time period for which you have decided to trade. When multiple positions are opened and closed within the span of one trading day, it is referred to as day trading, whereas swing trading might span over a time period that is definitely more than one day. The amount of capital available with a trader, the market they want to trade in, and their psychology plays a great role in deciding whether they want to go with swing trading or day trading.

I am not saying that any one of the trading styles is better than the other. What I am trying to say here is that the trading style which you will opt for has to suit your personal circumstances and thus, it is different for each and every person. There are some traders who love to do both at the same time, while some prefer sticking to any one of them. Now, we are going to discuss these two styles of trading with respect to certain factors, as mentioned below.

Potential Returns

If you are a trader who is looking for returns that have the ability to get compounded rapidly, then day trading is something that is suited for you what you want. Let us say that for every trade, you have agreed to risk 0.5% of your entire capital. So, if you lose that trade, then you will lose only 0.5% of the capital, but in the event that you win, you will make 1%. Do you know why? It is because of the 2:1 reward-to-risk ration of day trading.

Now, let us assume that you are going to win half of your trades, that is, 50%, and if on an average, you make 6 trades a day, then the amount being added to your account balance will be 1.5% every day minus the trading fees. Even if your growth is just 1% a day, over the course of one year, your account will have grown by 200% uncompounded.

On the other hand, you must also know that it is not that easy as it seems to be. Winning half the trades and also making twice on winning trades as compared to the losing trades is something that doesn't happen like a cakewalk. It's true that day trading can give you quick gains, but on the flip side, you have to remember that day trading can also deplete your account in an instant.

Now, let us talk about swing trading. In this case, your gains and losses both will take more time to accumulate as compared to day trading. But even after that, there can be swing trades that will give you huge gains and losses as well. Let us say we implement the same risk management ratio as mentioned above, and for every trade, we are risking 0.5% of the total capital. Your goal is to make a profit of at least 2% or 1% on your winning trades.

Let us say, for the losing trades, you lose 0.5%, but for the winning trades, you win 1.5% on an average. You are making six trades in 1 month, and you are winning half of them, which means 3. So, if we are to consider any random month, then the net profit on the account balance for a swing trader could be 3% minus the trading fees. And if you think about the entire year, then this will amount to 36% which is definitely much more than what a day trades has the potential to earn.

I hope that the above two examples have already illustrated to you the ways in which both these trading styles are different. The earning potential of any strategy will be drastically affected when you alter the average loss as compared to average win, percentage of winning trades, or even the number of trades performed. But if we are to consider this generally, then the profit potential is more in the case of day trading. It definitely holds true for smaller accounts, but with an increase in the size of the account, utilizing the capital becomes even tougher in the case of short-term day trades.

It is a known fact that when the capital of the day traders is more, the percentage of returns usually decreases. If you consider the dollar returns, then it still might be on the upwards side because 20% of $100,000 is still less than 5% of $1 million. In the case of swing trades, there is not a high chance of any such thing happening.

Requirements of Capital

The trading market is what defines the amount of capital required. The capital with which you are going to start your career in swing trading or day trading will differ and mostly depend on what you are trading – futures, forex, or stock.

If you are a day trader in the US, then there is a minimum account balance requirement that you have to meet, and that is - $25,000. But in the case of swing trading, there is no such minimum requirement. However, it is advised that your swing trading account should have at least $10,000 in it, and if you are looking forward to a sustainable income, then it should have at least $20,000.

There is no legal minimum amount required if you want to invest in the forex market as a day trader. But if you ask me, then my advice would be that you start with a minimum investment of $500 and it would be even better with $1,000. The preferable amount is obviously more, but you can start with these amounts. On the other hand, if you want to invest in the forex market as a swing trader, then I would recommend you start with an initial capital of $1,50, but here too, the preferable amount is much more than this. Do you know why I am asking you to invest more capital? It is because that will allow you to get into multiple trades at a time, thus increasing your chances of a good return.

Now, if you want to invest in futures as a day trader, you should start with something in the range of

$5,000-7,000, and the more you invest, the better. But, the futures contract that is involved in the trade will place a great impact on the amount to invest. In some cases, the type of contract might require you to invest way more capital than what I just said. But in case the contract is a micro-type, then you would not be needed that much amount of capital.

If you want to invest in futures as a swing trader, a sum in the range of $10,000-20,000 is required as an initial investment. Every contract being traded has its own margin requirement, and that is what varies the initial investment needed in a trade.

Trading Times

Both types of trading have their own times. You already know that day trading is all about trades being conducted on the same day, whereas swing trading, on the other hand, takes up more than one day. At an average, the time for trading for a day trader is two hours every day. Apart from the actual trading process, you have to consider the times for doing research, checking charts, reviews information, and so on, and so the time easily becomes three to four hours on the computer. And this is the minimum amount. If the time spent on trading is increased from two hours every day to a higher number, then the total time spent on trading also increases subsequently. So, it more or less becomes like a full-time job.

Now, if we are to discuss swing trading, it does not really require that much amount of time. Even if we consider the fact that you want to swing trade every day, updating orders and finding new trades is not going to take up much time for you and possibly about forty-five minutes every night. In fact, you do not even have to perform all of these activities every day. Swing trades can sometimes take weeks or months to complete, and you only have to take time out once a week to find new trades or update your current orders. So, I hope now you can understand that the commitment required in day trading is way more than swing trading.

Another thing that you should know that every action related to day trading is performed when the market is open, and that is during the day. Only a specific period of a day is meant for effective day trading. In case those hours of the day are not possible in your schedule, then I think swing trading might be a better alternative for you. The best thing in the case of swing trading is that there is no fixed time for you to look for the trades. You can place your orders whenever you like, and there is no barrier on the time which means that placing trades is possible even after the market has closed down.

The price changes occur every second, but the swing trades are not so easily affected by these minute changes. In the case of swing trading, you should be more concerned about the bigger picture. But in the case of day traders, every small change in price is important to you mainly because the trade has to happen in the span of one day, and you have to remain involved in the market at all times because you have to use these second-by-second movements in your favor.

Commitment and Practice

Both day trading and swing trading require you to possess a lot of knowledge and work experience in order to make good money from your trades. But you don't really have to be that 'bookish' person in order to excel. What I mean by knowledge is that you should be aware of the strategies to be used.

Moreover, you also need to have some amount of knowledge on the market in which you are trading because it plays a great role too and you also require lots of practice in that market in order to fully understand it. If you think that prices are going to move in the same manner throughout, then you are wrong because the prices are never the same. If today they are moving in a certain manner, tomorrow they will be moving in some other manner. So, even after you have figured out what strategy to use, you have to be able to implement that strategy in all types of market conditions that arise in front of you. You have to be highly adaptable to the conditions of the market and adjust your strategies and moves accordingly.

So, if you want consistent results even after so many barriers, then you have to keep practicing your strategies in different types of market conditions. This is not going to happen overnight, and it will take you a lot of time. That is why you should start with paper trading. We will discuss this more in the next section.

Your personality is another factor that you should take into consideration before making your decision regarding which type of trading you want to do. Your focus has to be more sustained in the case of day trading, and you will be under more stressful situations. It also takes an incredible amount of discipline, and you have to be on the market for an extended period of time too. So, if you have fast reflexes, have good actions, or if you like video games, then you are most likely to prefer day trading. But if you are someone who prefers to move at a slower pace and you want to maintain sufficient time between entering and exiting markets, then swing trading is what you should opt for. But don't get me wrong – swing trading might not be as active as day trading but it will still require you to be patient and disciplined. In the case of swing trading, you don't necessarily have to possess any fast reflexes because you are not time-bound. You can place your trades even after the market has closed.

But in both these types of trading, you are getting your own freedom because there is no one on top of you. You can work on your own, and for any of the profit or loss that is generated, it is you who is responsible. Yes, I know what you might be thinking that when it comes to time, it is the swing traders who have a greater amount of freedom.

Lastly, after making this comparison, I would like to remind you that neither of the styles is better than the other. They simply have different characteristics and are suited to varying needs.

Day Trading Restrictions That You Should Know About

SEC or Securities and Exchange Commission has set certain rules and restrictions on anyone who wants to practice day trading in the U.S. The main reason behind this is to limit the pattern day traders unless and until their trading account has an equity balance of $25,000 at least. In simpler terms, if you want to be able to day trade regularly in the U.S., this is the amount that your trading account should have.

What Is Pattern Day Trading?

I know many of you might not be aware of the term pattern day trading, and that is why I am going to explain what it is. According to the SEC, any trade will be categorized as a day trade when it has been opened and closed in the span of a single trading day. And when four or more than four trades have been conducted in a span of 5 trading days, it is referred to as pattern day trading. So, mathematically, out of the total trades in that 5-day period, 6% have to be day trades. And if you fall into this category, a minimum balance of $25,000 is mandatory in your trading account.

But this was just a definition made by SEC; sometimes, the rules are stringent with individual stockbrokers. Sometimes, this minimum balance is imposed even on those who are making two or three trades in that 5-day trading period, which simply means that if you want to day trade at all, your trading account should have $25,000.

What Happens If You Do Not Have $25,000 In Your Trading Account?

I know most of you might be thinking of this, so I want to clarify the confusion right away. If you are a pattern day trader by SEC's guidelines or by the guidelines set by your broker, you are required to have this minimum balance, and in case you don't have it, then you will not be allowed to make any more trades. Until and unless you increase the balance of your trading account to $25,000, the day trading option will be unavailable to you. Also, you have to understand that the minimum balance is required to be present in your account on the day of your trade. If you have less than that on other days, it does not really matter. What matters that on the day of trading, your account balance should be $25,000 at minimum.

What's the Leverage Here?

A 4:1 leverage is allowed for day traders in the U.S. If I have to break it down to you, it means that you are allowed to have $120,000 worth of positions accumulated if your account balance is $30,000. But if you had held the positions overnight, then the leverage is increased to 2:1. Since the positions of the day-traders are short-term, they are given more leverage. So, if you compare the trades with those which are held over an extended period of time, day trades are usually accustomed to experiencing smaller swings in price.

All That You Need to Know About Paper Trading

Remember when I told you about trying paper trading before coming into the real market? Well, now I am going to explain what it is all about. When you are new to the market, it is very natural for you to struggle and even make mistakes. And that is why it is better for every beginner to give their strategies a trial run before you actually implement them in the real world, and that is what paper trading is all about – it will give you the opportunity to try out the market without losing any money.

So, you will be taking hypothetical trades. You will write your buy and sell orders, and then you have to see how you would have performed if you were to execute it in the real world. If you want, you can even maintain a spreadsheet of the buy and sell orders and make the tracking process easier. But even for this, you should have your trading plan ready otherwise, you will not be able to know whether your plan is going to work out or not. Do your research and do everything like you would have done if it were real. Once your plan is ready, note down your entry point, and you have to take it as a filled order when that price is hit by the market. After that, you have to have a clear idea of how you want to exit the market and you should also have your stop-loss order ready.

If you want to stay really honest, then you should write down everything. After your exit has been hit, check whether you made a profit or a loss. Once you have done this for a couple of times, you will start to see whether you are fit for trading in the real world or whether you need some more practice.

Paper trading is only going to teach you how your strategies would have performed if you would have applied them in the real world, but you have to keep in mind that in the real world, there are a lot of other factors that play a role as well – the major one being your emotions. Trading psychology is an important aspect that you have to learn, and we are going to go through it in Chapter 9. I know that paper trading is never going to give you the complete experience but it is somewhat a necessity and you should do it before putting your actual capital at risk.

Chapter 8:

HOW TO MAKE A TRADE?

If you want to get started with placing trades, you first have to determine which companies you want to invest in. The industry you select should be something that you are well-familiar with, but the company has to be selected after considerable research. The best way to do it is by performing fundamental analysis. It is basically a technique that will help you to understand a company's potential to keep generating dividends in the upcoming years.

Some of the things that fundamental analysis will help you answer are –

- Are the profits shown by the company along the same lines as their growth?

- Has the company paid all its debts?

- Is the company currently making substantial

profits?

- Is the revenue of the company moving in a direction that is profitable for you?

- Is the framework of the company strong enough to carry on its potential even in the upcoming years and generate good profits?

I know these are quite extensive questions, but once you get the answer to them, it will become clear to you whether the company will be a good investment for you or not. We will discuss fundamental analysis in detail in my next books on different trading methods. But something that you should understand is that if you are a day trader, then fundamental analysis is not going to be of much importance because of the sole reason that your trades are for the short-term. The balance sheet of a company is not really going to matter so much for a trade that lasted only for 5 minutes. Let us say a company's financials are horrible, but in the case of a trade conducted for the span of a single day, those financials won't matter because you are looking for small fluctuations in price. Similarly, a company might be performing very well for months and paying high dividends to the shareholders and yet it can make you suffer a loss in the case of day trading. When the trade is about such a short period of time, basically anything can happen. And if you spend your time focusing on the fundamentals, you will only be looking in the wrong direction.

So, then when is the fundamental analysis required? Well, anyone who is going to be in the market for a long-term needs to understand fundamental analysis. As a day trader, it will be more beneficial if you keep a close eye on the price movements in a day and check the price patterns.

Steps To Follow for Your First Trade

Now, let me take you on a step-by-step journey on how you can make your first trade.

Step 1 – Open the Trading Platform

I have already explained in Chapter 3 that you have to select your online broker and then open an account with them. In order to place your first trade, you have to open the platform.

Step 2 – Fund Your Account

The second step is quite obvious, but I am going to mention it anyway. If you do not fund your account, you won't be able to place any trades. So, start by transferring some cash into your account. You can choose an ACH bank transfer or a check to fund your account. If you want more specifics, then you can talk to the personnel responsible for this in the company. You will be ready for your trade as soon as your money is in your trading account. Another thing to keep in mind here is that certain types of trades require you to have a minimum account balance in order to be eligible to place those trades. You have to know them too; otherwise, you wouldn't know how much money you should transfer to your trading account. That is why the importance of research is paramount before you start trading.

Step 3 – Place Your Trade

In the next step, you have to place your trade. There are certain things that I am going to explain to you with respect to this step. There will be an option for 'Trades' in your brokerage account, and no matter what you want to trade, you have to visit this screen first. Once you have decided what to invest in, you have to select the position size or volume of the trade.

Selecting the volume of trade is one of the crucial steps because it is going to determine a lot of things. You have to keep in mind the different risk management rules before you select your position, and you are going to learn more about this in the next chapter. But one simple thing that you should know is that the larger the portion, the larger will be your loss or profit. But if you are to follow the rule of thumb, then you should not be risking more than 2% of your total trading account in any single trade. In this way, even if you lose, it will not be more than 2% of your trading account. So, you should risk only $20, if you have $1,000 in your trading account.

Step 4 – Set Stop Loss

It is very important that you fix the stop loss level; otherwise, you might end up losing a lot of money. It is not a mandatory step that without it, you won't be able to trade, but it is definitely an essential step for bringing home maximum profits.

In fact, setting a stop loss is something that every experienced trader is going to advise you to do. Let us say the market is not moving as you predicted it to move. In such a case, it will be the stop loss that will prevent you from incurring huge losses. There is another thing that you should set, and that is the take profit level, and because of this, you can take home the profits you expected when the market moves in a direction that you had predicted it to move. When you are in the market, the conditions are not always what you thought would be and so making the right decisions become strenuous. That is why if you set these levels beforehand, you will be making the right decisions and stick to your trading plan no matter what.

Step 5 – Order Confirmation

The next step is to wait for order confirmation. After you have submitted your order, the confirmation will pop up on the screen. It is very important because it will give you a reference number which you will need in case you have to contact the broker regarding something related to this particular trade. By this, I do not mean that something wrong usually happens, but it is just that you should be prepared for every possible situation so that if it does happen, you stay prepared with everything you might need to solve it. In fact, if a mistake is made and your broker has to rectify it, then your broker will want to see this reference number, and if need be, then refund your account.

Step 6 – Complete the Trade

The next step is when you complete the trade. For this, your exit strategy should be in place, and you have to stick with your exit strategy. Sometimes, traders exit too early or too late, both of which might result in a loss or a lesser profit and these scenarios are avoidable only if you learn to manage your emotions. We are going to discuss this in more detail in the next chapter.

Create a Trading Routine

If you have started trading, then you should also set up a routine that you will follow diligently. Having a routine will mitigate mistakes. When you are in the market, you might have too much information in your hand that can become difficult to handle. And that is why if you have a routine, you will continue to follow an automated cycle and make some tweaks here and there depending on the market condition. If you have this pre-trading checklist or routine ready in your hands, then all you have to do is simply check it out the night before your trading day. It will only take you a couple of minutes, but it has the ability to save you from a lot of frustration the next day.

A typical trading routine should look something like this –

Always Refer to Your Economic Calendar

The prices of assets can be greatly influenced by certain economic events in a year like the annual budget or elections. So, if you are in that time of the year where some high-impact event is going to take place, or important news is about to be announced, it is best that you do not trade on that day. That is why it is important that you refer to your economic calendar prior to your trading day. In case you are regularly trading individual stocks, then you should also keep a close check on any news related to the company that might affect the stocks.

Open the Platform

The next thing that you should do is check whether the platform is functioning properly or not. The quotes should not be sporadic or lagging. In fact, they should always be streaming. The data feeds offered by most brokers are trustable, but you should always be careful and keep an eye out. If anything seems fishy or if you feel that the feed seems to be inaccurate, then you should report it to your broker at once.

Trade the Correct Contract and Account

People sometimes have multiple accounts for trading, and they also have simulated accounts where they practice trading. Make sure you didn't get confused between them and place your trade in the wrong account. This is something that happens to people and that is why I am asking you to be wary of it. If you placed the trade in the simulation account and at the end of the day when you think your day was so much profitable, you will come to know that you had not actually got any profits because the trade was placed in a simulated account. Also, if you are trading futures on a regular basis, then the contract you are choosing has to be cross-checked to ensure that you have chosen the correct one. The contracts also come with expiration dates and before you trade them, make sure you check the dates.

Maintain Text Notes

Make it a practice to put up text notes on your chart; for example, you can mention when any major news release is going to happen. This is important because you might have become so engrossed in your trade that you forgot to check the time and missed the important announcement time, which might result in losses if the market moved in the opposite direction. So, if there is anything that you want yourself to be reminded of, write it down on your chart.

You have to figure out when the approximate time of the announcement would be and put up the note accordingly. In this way, you will become aware of it when the time comes.

Always Check Your Automated Strategies

There will always be certain automated order even when you are trading manually. For example, a stop-loss order can be automated in various broker platforms, and if you have selected such an option, make sure you triple-check these things.

Check Your Default Position Size

If you are someone who prefers to trade with a default position size, then you have to keep a close eye on it too. Your position size can impact a lot of things, and an extra zero can make the whole world of difference in it. And if you drop a digit from the default size, then your trade reduces by a fraction of the original amount, and you will end up missing out a great opportunity to make profits.

On the other hand, if you are into manual trading where you enter the position size manually as well, you should check your account balance before doing that.

Lastly, I would advise you to maintain a trading journal where you will be noting down everything. This will give you a great learning opportunity. Even if you end up making mistakes, it will be noted in the journal, and in this way, you will be able to learn from the mistakes you make. If any similar situation arises, you will know what to do.

Chapter 9:
RISK MANAGEMENT AND TRADING PSYCHOLOGY

There is a very crucial relationship between return and risk in the stock market, and you have to understand this if you want to venture into risk management. The return is usually more when the risk is more. If we are to see the financial terminology, then risk management is basically about identifying the risk, assessing it, and then designing strategies that will help you mitigate the risk. While you are minimizing the risk, your focus should also be on how you can maximize the returns.

A certain amount of risk is associated with every investment or trade you make in the stock market, and this is inevitable. And as an investor, your duty is to assess this risk and figure out whether the trade that you are making can equally compensate for this risk or not. In short, this will help you determine whether the trade that you are about to conduct would be logical for the risk that you are taking. The compensation that we are talking about has a particular term, and it called simply premium or risk premium. So, a central part of stock market investing is the factor of risk and you cannot expect any gains if you are not willing to undertake this risk. Risk management strategies are used by successful investors to maximize their profits and minimize their risk.

Types of Risk

When we are talking about the stock market, there are different types of risk involved and not just one. Before moving on to the strategies of mitigating this risk, let us discuss more about the types of risk.

Market Risk

This is the most basic type of risk in the stock market, and it refers to the possibility of losing money due to the overall performance of the financial market. Sometimes, the term systematic risk is also used to refer to market risk. Market risk is something that you cannot eliminate even if you diversify your portfolio. You have to deal with this kind of risk through hedging. We are going to come to it in the latter part of this chapter. Market risk can arise in different situations and some of those situations are –

- Political turmoil
- Changes in interest rates
- Recession
- Terrorist attacks
- Natural calamities

When this kind of risk occurs, it is not any one company or sector that is influenced, but the entire economy is affected. Market risks are more in short-term investments and trades rather than the long-term ones.

Business Risk

The next time of risk that you have to face if you set foot in the stock market is business risk. It mainly comes from the business, as you might have understood from the term. The different factors to which a company is exposed to, which can cause a fall in the price of its stocks is referred to as business risk. This risk can be constituted by anything and everything that might be a threat to the growth of the company. There are different sources from which business risk might arise. And if you think that the head of the company is the person who is to be blamed for this, then you are wrong – it is often not the case. Instead, it can be some regulation that was made in the economy or it might be some internal reason as well.

It's true that no company can completely shelter itself from facing business risk, but you, as an investor, should be aware of the fact when a company is more likely to face this kind of risk. If you misjudge a company and overlook the aspect of business risk that they might be facing, then you will have to pay for it dearly. This is where diversification of investments comes in and we will learn about it later.

Liquidity Risk

One of the prime requisites of stock market investing is that you should always check how much solvent a company is before investing in its stocks. The bills of a company will not be paid smoothly if it is already submerged in debts. In fact, in order to clear those debts, the company might cut off the dividends, and that is where you are going to make losses. And if the conditions worsen, the company might even go bankrupt.

Taxability Risk

The tax rules keep changing from time to time, and you have to stay updated with all of them if you want to invest in the stock market. It is because of these changing rules, the tax that you have to pay for the investments might increase or even decrease. The prices of stocks are also affected by any change in the taxation policies.

Another thing to keep in mind is that when certain industries have to pay a higher amount of tax as compared to the others, they incur a much lesser amount of profit, and so, this is something that you should keep an eye on. And the management of those companies cannot really do much about taxation since the rules here are set by the government.

Interest Rate Risk

The interest rates in the global market undergo fluctuations all the time. Now, the direction of the movement of these interest rates will determine whether your investment has been affected positively or negatively. A company will not be able to borrow money when it needs it because of high-interest rates. Also, with an increase in interest rate, the bond market suffers, and it leaves a direct impact on corporate bonds as well.

Regulatory Risk

Next, we are going to discuss the regulatory risk involved while you are investing in stocks. This kind of risk might differ from one industry to another because the regulations imposed might be industry-specific too. For example, some industries like telecommunication, pharma, and cigarettes are highly regulated at all times, and you should keep up with any new changes because they can directly impact your investment. Let us say there was some new regulation released because of which the drug manufacturing permission of a pharma company was revoked. What do you think will happen to its stock price? It will see a steep decline.

Inflationary Risk

As you know that inflation is a risk that is present with every type of investment you make. Although stock markets are where you can invest your money to overcome inflation, you will still face it. Some companies that are mostly affected by the inflationary risk are those that are selling commodities. In certain sectors, the inflation rate is more than the others, and these are – healthcare and education.

Other Risks

Some other risks that you should be aware of are definitely the political risks that can come out of nowhere and influence the price of stocks. Then there is exchange rate risk for companies who have overseas branches, and an increase in currency exchange rates would harm them directly.

If you are overwhelmed after knowing about all these different types of risks, then let me tell you something – these risks have been present in the stock market ever since, and people have still been making profits. This is because there is a solution for every risk, and we are going to learn those risk management strategies in the next section.

Risk Management Strategies That You Should Know

Most traders do not prioritize risk management on their to-do list, but it is something that should be taken with seriousness; otherwise, it will be you who will suffer huge losses. Profitable trading will become easier when you have a better knowledge of mitigating risks. If you are not sure how to go about it, then here are some basic strategies that you should know about.

Diversify Your Investment Sectors

Allocating your investment capital in different sectors is the first thing that you should do, and this process is known as diversification. It is similar to not putting all your trades in one basket. The main aim is that even if the market undergoes a change, you have to diversify your capital in such a way that each of these sectors reacts to the change in a different way. I would not lie to you – diversification is not something that will guarantee no loss at all, but it is definitely a great strategy for minimizing all the risks involved.

Let me give you an example, and it will become clear as to what I am trying to say. Suppose you have bought stocks in the airline industry, and all your stocks are from this sector. What will happen if, for some reason, the airline staff raises a strike? The stock prices will suffer and you will incur huge losses because all your stocks are from here. But what if you also purchased some stocks in the railway sector? This will mean that your risk gets balanced. When the workers of the airlines go on a strike, the flights will not operate as usual and the people will turn to railways for travel which would increase their revenue and also their stock price. This type of relation is called correlation in the world of statistics.

Your portfolio should also contain different types of investment classes like bonds, stocks, gold, real estate, cash, and so on. When only one asset is present in your portfolio, it will suffer more. It is true that if you had only stocks in your portfolio, it would have the potential to rise faster, but it is also true that having different classes of assets will reduce the risk of losing all your money.

Let me give you a real-world example of why you need to diversify. At the turn of the millennium, people had heavily invested in Amazon. In fact, the shares of Amazon were being sold at $100 in the month of December in 2000. But in October 2001, the stocks went down to as low as $6, and anyone who depended only on those stocks must have had a very bad loss. The stocks had returned back to the range of $90 only in 2007. Do you see the gap?

Until now, you only saw all the advantages of diversification. There are certain disadvantages that you should know, as well. One of the major downsides of a diverse portfolio is that you have to manage a lot of things, and you might not have the time or patience to do that. The second disadvantage is that not every investment costs the same. Some of them might have more costs associated with them than the other. And everything starting from brokerage costs to transaction fees can eat away your profits. No matter how much you spend on analysis, no one can guarantee any investment to be 100% profitable. There will always be a risk of loss but diversification can help you reduce that risk a bit.

Avoid Any Type of Earnings Surprise

Anyone who has ever invested in the stock market knows that the time prior to any announcement related to earnings is when everyone tenses up. It is because it is a period of uncertainty that can change everything for you. But does it have to be like that?

I know what you are assuming – that positive earnings are something you should look for, but no, positive earnings can be dangerous too. The major earnings surprises usually happen with penny stocks. These stocks are low in price, which is why most beginners invest in them, but they are also from shady companies or companies that are much riskier to invest in. In such cases, it becomes nearly unpredictable whether the company is going to perform well in the future or whether it is going to face a downward spiral.

Some of the signs that will show you a company is

going to provide an earnings surprise (both good and bad) are as follows –

- If the stock has been covered by a limited number of analysts, say one or two.

- The company does not have much experience or is brand new, and so you do not have much historical data in your hand to judge its past performance. And that is why it becomes difficult to gauge the future earnings of the company as well.

- If the analysis that you have received from different analysts is full of inconsistencies, then you should exercise uncertainty regarding the future of the company.

But one thing is clear – when the analysis reports are consistent, and when the earnings of a company have been accurately reported over the course of the past few years, you can stay assured about the future of the company.

Don't Rely on Daily Performance Targets

If you are into trading and you have this habit of setting daily targets for yourself, then you have to stop doing that because it is going to give you nothing but harm. When you start thinking in terms of daily income, you will have the urge to invest more than you should. You have to remember that the stock market is not about what you are getting on a daily basis. This kind of mentality can create the need for trade in your mind even when all the external factors suggest that you should not put your money in the market now. You have to think long-term.

Steps to Master Trading Psychology

Before we go into any further details, let us first understand what trading psychology is. If you have come to this part of the book, you already know that in order to become a successful trader, you have to master a lot of skills. You have to determine the direction of price movement, and you also have to determine whether the company in whose stocks assets you are investing in is actually in good health. But one thing that you forget here is that a trader's mindset is possibly the greatest skill that needs to be polished. Successful traders can think quickly and make strong decisions even when they are under a lot of pressure. They do not bow down to their emotions and this is something that you have to learn. All of this falls under trading psychology.

There are basically two basic emotions that can

hamper with your trade and through the different steps of trading psychology, you will learn how to get these two emotions under your control –

- **Greed** – The first emotion is greed. Let's say your trade is performing well and you have made a good amount of money. The time has come for you to exit the trade, but you chose to stay because you wanted more profits. This is greed, and you never know when the market will turn in the opposite direction and you will incur a huge loss. The emotion of greed is not an easy one to overcome but if you keep at it, you will be successful.

- **Fear** – The next emotion that you should be aware of is fear. It is very common to receive some sort of bad news in the middle of a trade. But that is when you cannot let your fear cloud your judgment. No matter what happens, you have to make the right decisions. If you feel that you have to liquidate your stocks just because there was some random announcement, take a step back and think whether it is really a sane decision to make. Sometimes, you need to learn to quantify your fear, and maybe that will help you deal with it. Thinking of your trading ahead of time and having a trading plan ready is definitely one of the effective ways of dealing with fear.

Once you master these emotions, you can overcome a lot of hurdles on your path to become a successful trader.

Get In the Right Mindset

There are so many self-motivation exercises that will help you stay motivated as a trader. You should also consider giving yourself a pep talk whenever you feel demotivated. It doesn't have to be anything elaborate. Simple things like reminding yourself not to take a fall in stock prices personally can make you feel a lot better.

You should also give yourself enough time to come into a balanced state of mind. If you wake up at 8:02 am and expect yourself to concentrate on trading right away, then that is where your mistake lies. You won't be able to remain level-headed like this. You should try to wake up a bit earlier. You can even set your own morning ritual that will help you concentrate. You are a human being, and so completely eliminating your emotions from the picture is something that you definitely cannot do but what you can do is reduce any potential damage to your calm mindset.

Enhance Your Knowledge Base

When you have researched properly, you automatically become more confident and panic less. This will ensure that you make the right decisions along the way. No matter what curveballs are thrown at you, your technical prowess will help you move forward. That is why educating yourself about everything related to the stock market, and your particular line of trading is so important and something that you should skip on. Once you do it, you will make more informed decisions than before.

Visualize Yourself Winning

Visualization is a great exercise in every sphere of life, including trading. Visualizing a win can actually keep you motivated and drive you to move towards the goal with greater vigor. You can even create a visualization board of your financial goals and stick pictures of things that resemble your dream. Keep the board somewhere you can see it easily every day. When you imagine the best case scenario about something, you will automatically be pushing yourself to move towards the positive.

Tell Yourself That It's Real Money

When you are trading in the stock market, you are not seeing any real cash, and that is why some traders do not find any motivation or do not take it seriously. It has been noticed that traders feel better and more motivated towards their goal when they keep some real money on the table. When they see that physical cash, they automatically feel the stakes and realize that it is real money that they are dealing with and not some numbers on a screen.

Keep Practicing

You are not going to become a very successful trader overnight. There is a lot to learn in the world of stocks, and it will take time. Until then, you have to keep practicing by placing trades and implementing the strategies that you have built. This will help you to hone your skills. With time, you will also gain a greater amount of mental strength to actually carry on with the strategies that you have devised and not falter when the market does not move the way you predicted it to.

Observe Your Progress

After a certain period of time, monitor how far you have come since the beginning and how much progress you have made. I am going to say this again – a trading journal is one of the best ways in which you can keep track of your progress. If you are not willing to write, you can maintain a document on your phone or even your laptop. The main aim is to document everything, and it does not really matter whether you do it physically or digitally. Your journal will become an invaluable source to you over the course of the years.

Now that you know some of the tips to control your emotions and improve your trading strategies over time, you have to understand that your emotions are very fickle. If you are having a profitable trade now, you will feel happy and confident, but things don't take much time to go south, and the moment it does, you will feel weighed down and start panicking. That is the moment you have to tell yourself that it is okay and you can still make up for it some other day. Lastly, don't be too hard on yourself. Everyone makes mistakes and mistakes are exactly how you are going to learn.

Chapter 10:
Mistakes That You Should Avoid

If you are looking for high returns, then the stock market is definitely the right place for it, but at the same time, there are certain mistakes that can totally destroy what you have built so far. In this chapter, we are going to discuss some of those mistakes so that when you know them from before, you will become aware of them and not make them yourselves.

Also, you should know that mistakes are not that much of a rare occurrence and it happens with everyone. Even if you ask the most established investor in the stock market, they will tell you the same things. Everyone has made mistakes, but what is important is that you learn from those mistakes.

No Basic Knowledge

Before you start investing in stocks, there is some basic knowledge that you should have. Otherwise, it will be the same as walking in the dark. And people who lack sufficient knowledge are exactly the ones who end up losing a lot of money when they do come into the market. When you are not experienced, and you haven't gathered knowledge about what usually happens at the exchange, you are at a greater risk of paying exaggerated prices for stocks that could have been grabbed at much lower prices. This is because when you don't have the knowledge, you don't know even the most basic things and factors that determine the prices of stocks and neither do you know anything about buying and selling stocks. So, before you make any purchases, you've got introduce yourself by researching and gaining basic knowledge.

You have to know how the stock market works and how the price of stocks is fixed. You also have to know about the basic terms, and then you have to gain knowledge about setting up your own portfolio. If you think that you can just wing it while you are on the exchange floor, then you have got it all wrong.

Investing In An Industry You Don't Know About

Whenever you hear about a certain industry or business making it big in the stock market, I know what you might be thinking – you think why not try your hand at it, right? Well, you see that's where the problem lies. No matter how fancy an industry might seem to you, it will not do you any good to invest in that industry if you do not know it well. Let us say, you hear some company in the biotech industry is doing good, but you don't have any knowledge about biotech whatsoever, should you invest in it? No. Why? I will explain it here.

Have you ever thought about what advantage you will have when you invest in an industry that you know everything about? You will automatically have the upper hand over other investors in that same industry who know nothing about it. In fact, when someone knows everything about an industry, you have this advantage over other investors. By extension of this, you will automatically be more aware of when the industry is slowing down, booming, or suffering from a setback. And you are going to know all of this before the majority of the other investors in the market which is going to get you the best deals. When you are the first to notice certain trends in the industry, you are also in a better position to make good investment decisions.

On the other hand, you will be missing out on most subtleties if you invest in a company belonging to a market that you know nothing about. You will not be able to grasp the complexities involved, and this will put you in a bad position. I am certainly not implying that in order to invest in the healthcare industry, you have to be a doctor, but you definitely got to possess some knowledge.

You have to press an advantage whenever you have it over other investors. In simpler terms, whenever you are more aware of any certain industry or if you are working in that industry and investing in the stock market at the same time, then you already have an inside track of what is going on.

Having Too High Expectations

Beginners often have a lot of high expectations when they are investing in stocks. This becomes even more evident when we are talking about the penny stocks. Penny stocks are the ones that you can get for as low as $1, and beginners jump into them thinking that they can get a lot of them with a small amount of investment. In fact, they start treating these stocks as some kind of lottery. By investing so little, they expect they might make as high as $2000 but make no mistake; investing in stocks is not the same as gambling.

I am not saying that there are no odds, but that's exactly what they are – odds and they probably happen once in several years. So, would you incur huge losses by maintaining that mindset? This is not the kind of mindset that a successful investor should have in the first place. What you need to do is that you have to be realistic and not expect too much from the shares.

Start by analyzing the performance of the stock that you are dealing with and see how it has performed to date. You also need to check out what the competitors in the market are doing. If history is to be believed, then the stock market has proven itself to give not more than 5-10% of returns annually. So, is this percentage any close to the ones that you are expecting? If not, then you have to change your mindset. I am not saying that there are no exceptions. There can be years where this percentage is 15%, and there can also be years when it is 8$ but you have to stay realistic about what you expect.

If you analyze the previous performance of any particular company, you will get a rough idea about how much you should expect. And by this, I mean that you will be having a full idea of the trading activity and the volatility of the shares underneath. Generally, a stock does not deviate much from its past performances, and usually, this performance is along the same lines as the rest of the industry.

Investing With the Mindset of a Trader

You have to understand that there is a difference in being a trader to that of an investor. Like that saying about there are no free lunches in the world; you are not going to come into the stock market and become a billionaire overnight. That sort of thing only happens in movies. The stock market is not the place for you if all you want are quick gains. That is also how an investor differs from a trader. The main of a trader is to buy an asset and then sell it so that profit can be made in between, and an investor, on the other hand, believes in buying and investing. So, do you understand what the basic difference is? Investing is a long-term approach and it is of utmost importance that you learn the difference between investing and speculation.

If you are new into the stock market, then it is easy for you to get baffled by terms like cyclical movements and volatility, but if you have reached this part of the book then you have already learned those and if not, I would advise you to go back and read them. These are the basics of stocks and you cannot make profits without laying out your foundation. Now let us say you have recently invested your money in stocks but because of some geopolitical situation, the market is in bad shape and you are losing money. You think that taking out your money will save you from losses but that's the thing about investing. You have to keep your money for the long-term in order to truly witness profits.

There will always be ups and downs in the stock market, and that is quite natural. This is what the cyclical nature of the market is all about. If you want to make profits, keep your money invested for a long time and you are not going to regret it. The major mistake that leads to huge losses is an early redemption of your money.

The share price of a company's stocks is not going to grow until and unless the company itself starts growing. So, you have to give them sufficient time for that. Now, let us see what happens if you give in to your panic and fear – you sell your stocks and exit from the market in a rush, and your portfolio suffers, which, in turn, makes you lose your opportunity of growing your money in any way.

Becoming Emotionally Associated With a Company

You cannot let any of your emotions come in your way if you have to invest in the stock market in the right manner. We have already discussed how ruining your emotions can be for your profits, but I am going to tell you this again from a different perspective. You always have to keep an eye out for any type of red flags associated with a company, and that brings me to my next point – never trust any company blindly. Check their performance in every quarter and see whether any of the non-performing assets are showing the upward movement if someone from the senior leaders has exited abruptly.

In case you think you won't have the time to do all of this on your own or if you think you are not ready to do all the research on your own, you should consider taking professional help. Never chase the returns because there are other factors regarding the company that should be looked into. Sometimes the high returns that you are getting are simply because of a bull run that is momentary. What needs even more attention is the business model and growth objectives of the company. You have to remember that even if you are seeing high valuations now if the company fails to keep up on other factors, the stock price is eventually going to come down.

Investing Money That Is Too Important to Lose

Remember how at the beginning book, I told you that if you are going to come into the stock market, you've got to have an emergency fund and your day-to-day expenses figured out. You cannot trade or invest the money that you cannot afford to lose, but this is also the kind of mistake that beginners make. This is also how your stress levels become high, and your emotions are heightened and the cumulative effect of all of this is that you take the wrong decisions. So, if you need the money for other reasons that are important, why invest it in the stock market in the first place? This is because that would be like putting yourself in a stressful situation deliberately when you could have avoided it altogether.

That is why I always suggest beginners get used to the stock market through paper trading, which involved no risk at all. Once you think you are doing well, you can move into real cash, but only after you have managed other expenses. You will be able to see the difference for yourself. When you are investing money that is not of maximum importance, your trading decisions will be way relaxed and you won't panic. Since your actions are no longer driven by fear or any kind of negative emotions, you will be making better decisions.

Not Diversifying Enough

I have already stressed the importance of diversification in the previous chapter, but I am going to say it again – diversification is something that will help you keep a lot of risks at bay and if you think about omitting on diversification, you are truly making the biggest mistake. In fact, not engaging in sufficient diversification is probably the commonest blunder made by beginner investors. Let us say that you have invested in twenty different stocks, among which 10 are based in the tech industry while the rest of the ten are in energy companies. Do you think your portfolio is diversified? No, it's not. If there is a recession in the tech market, then your portfolio is going to take a major hit, and similarly, if the prices of gas or oil changes, then your portfolio is going to get affected to a huge extent.

So, your aim should be investing your money across several different industries so that none of the industries are too much invested in and hold the power to impact your portfolio to a great extent. If you are from the U.S., you should definitely focus on the U.S. stocks but don't turn a complete blind eye to the international stocks because they are equally important. You also have to keep in mind that there are several U.S. companies that have considerably big foreign operations.

Another thing that you have to keep in mind is that you cannot put all your money in stocks because that is exactly what putting all your eggs in one basket means. So, your portfolio should be a perfect mixture of bonds, stocks, equities, cash assets, and fixed income.

Buying Shares On Credit

This is another mistake that you should be aware of so that you don't end up doing it yourself. There are several professionals who buy shares on credit. They approach a broker or a bank so that they will lend them money for purchasing shares. Once there is an increase in the price of the share, they sell those shares, and repay the debt to the lender. They make a profit from the difference. But think about a situation where there was no increase in the share price? What would you do then? If the price of the share falls instead of rising, the broker or the bank from whom you have borrowed the money will expect you to pay them back a greater amount. This is a margin call, and this is exactly what leads to a greater amount of loss when compared to the investment you made.

Sometimes, people who are starting out in the stock market don't approach banks, but they approach their friends and family members for lending them money. But in case such an investment does not turn out the way you expected it to, you don't have to pay them a higher interest like the bank, but you will be left with broken relationships. So, steer clear of equity trading on credit. If you incur losses, you will be devastated. The stakes are too high to take such a risk and it won't be worth it.

No matter how many mistakes you face in trading or investing in the stock market, you have to learn from your mistakes, and don't worry; you will quickly phase-out of this. In fact, these mistakes will enhance your wisdom making sure that you don't fall for the same traps again.

CONCLUSION

Thank you for making it through to the end of *Stock Market Investing for Beginners*, let's hope it was informative and able to provide you with all of the tools you need to achieve your goals whatever they may be.

The next step is to implement these lessons in real life. Remember that your win rate is not everything. If you are just a beginner, research a lot, and learn the basics before you place your first trade. There is nothing more dangerous than incomplete knowledge. Don't forget to adjust your risk levels for every trade so that you are not risking too much. Don't trade too much at a stretch. Take regular breaks; otherwise, you are going to get bogged down by the stress.

When you are taking off time from trading, you can spend your time learning about newer strategies or other forms of investment. Update your trading journal even on the days when you are not trading.

Maintain discipline and patience because these two qualities are of utmost importance in a trader. Improve your money management skills and remain realistic and logical. Don't trust random tips and don't believe everything that you watch on TV. Do your own research. I would like to wish you all the best in your new endeavor, and I hope you meet all your financial goals.

Finally, if you found this book useful in any way, a review on Amazon is always appreciated!

Other Book by Robert Winston Moore jr:

OPTIONS TRADING FOR BEGINNERS: THE STEP-BY-STEP CRASH COURSE TO MAKE MONEY AND CREATE A PASSIVE INCOME BY OPTIONS TRADING JUST A FEW MINUTES A DAY

If you want to learn how to make weekly and monthly income with options trading, then read on.

I know, maybe you've already read books or watched hours and hours of videos on trading options, and yet something doesn't seem right.

Unclear methods, systems that don't work, time and money wasted.

When I started studying the world of trading it happened to me too, I know how you're feeling.

The world is full of *"gurus"*, who haven't generated a dollar of profit from the stock market and therefore cannot teach you how to do it.

This book is the result of many years of experience. *My family lives off the interest of this work of mine and I will teach you precisely and clearly the same techniques that I have been using to generate steady profits.*

I have decided to develop the **Moore Trading Method** so that *you will be able to read my books, start from scratch and become an expert trader with an annual income of five or six figures.*

This book will provide you the following benefits:

- **You will learn the basics and the terms you need to understand option trading**
- **All tricks to be successful**
- **Tips to keep in mind to become a top trader**

- How to start with little money
- How to earn when the market goes up, when it goes down and when it remains stable
- how to make weekly and monthly income with various options strategies
- You will see real examples for every step that will help you to learn how to trade options successfully
- You will learn, how to use leverage and fundamental analysis
- How to choose the best platforms for options
- You will know how to trade while minimizing risks
- I WILL teach you how to control your emotions and dominate the market
- This book has been made easy to read and understand

Even if you've already tried the options, maybe you've lost money and been disappointed.

It was not the options that didn't work, it was the method. This is why I hope that the ***Moore Trading Method*** can teach you a simple and profitable method.

Remember, Options are definitely the best starting point for becoming a good trader, it takes a few minutes a day and it can make you financially free.

You can buy on Amazon at this link:
https://www.amazon.com/dp/B0882HYBXH

www.ingramcontent.com/pod-product-compliance
Lightning Source LLC
Chambersburg PA
CBHW070412220526
45465CB00010B/370